Louis Landon

Healing Piano of Sedona for massage, yoga and relaxation

Healing Piano of Sedona is pianist/composer Louis Landon's fifteenth release and is a bit different from his previous albums in that this is music intended for massage, yoga and relaxation. While Landon has been involved in the so-called new age piano genre for close to ten years, he is an incredibly versatile artist with a strong background in jazz and improvisation. A life-long professional musician, Landon recently relocated from New York to Sedona, AZ and part of that move included starting Healing Piano of Sedona which offers "mentoring, music and sound vibrations that are personalized to assist you in your soul's journey." I don't know how much of the music on this album is improvised, but all twelve tracks are serene, smooth, and very free. Much of Landon's other music contains rather dense chords and the complex rhythms found in jazz, but this one is more like a gently flowing stream that moves at its own pace without being hurried or encumbered in any way. I've been listening to it in my car as well as in my office, and it's amazing how peaceful and contented it can make you feel whether it is in the background or you're listening with more focus. All of the pieces are about five minutes in length, which gives them plenty of time to evolve, develop and work their magic.

Healing Piano of Sedona begins with "Breath," a quietly understated piece that invites you to let go of your cares and give in to the soothing power of the music. "Sands of Time" is more melodic and lightly rhythmic. "Child Pose" has an innocent, playful attitude, with much of it played in the upper registers of the piano. "Harp Goddess" has more of the complicated chord patterns I would expect from Landon, but the delivery is silky-smooth. Although the two pieces are quite different from each other, both "Dream Weaver" and "Water Wheel" are driven by repetitive left hand patterns and very freely expressive right hands - both are very delicate and beautiful. "Perseverance" seems a bit more structured, although this is relative. It is one of my favorite tracks. "Garden of Eden" is heavenly - warm, peaceful, and blissful. Landon's piano touch on this piece is amazing! "Soaring" is my favorite of the twelve and vaguely resembles Landon's "Icicles" - one of my favorite Landon pieces ever! I hope this one becomes sheet music soon! "Shangri-La" brings the album to a serene and peaceful close with a little bit of paradise. Very free in both form and mood, it will end your one-hour session feeling refreshed, relaxed, and ready to tell the world that you are "excellent and better all the time!"

Louis Landon has had a longtime mission to to create a more loving and peaceful world by writing, recording and performing music from the heart and *Healing Piano of Sedona* will certainly take him even closer to his goal. It is available from www.louislandon.com, Amazon, iTunes, and CD Baby. Very highly recommended!

Kathy Parsons MainlyPiano.com

Healing Piano of Sedona
for massage, yoga and relaxation

sheet music for solo piano

1. Breathe..1
2. Sands of Time......................................5
3. Ascending Souls..................................9
4. Child's Pose..13
5. Harp Goddess.....................................18
6. Dream Weaver....................................21
7. Water Wheel.......................................24
8. Perseverance......................................28
9. Garden of Eden..................................32
10. Into the Depths.................................35
11. Soaring..38
12. Shangri-La..43

ISBN 978-0-9863062-8-0
©2016 Landon Creative, Inc.

Breathe

from the solo piano CD, *Healing Piano of Sedona for massage, yoga and relaxation*
Available from *www.louislandon.com*

LOUIS LANDON

Copyright © 2014 Landon Creative, Inc. (BMI)
International Copyright Secured. All Rights Reserved.

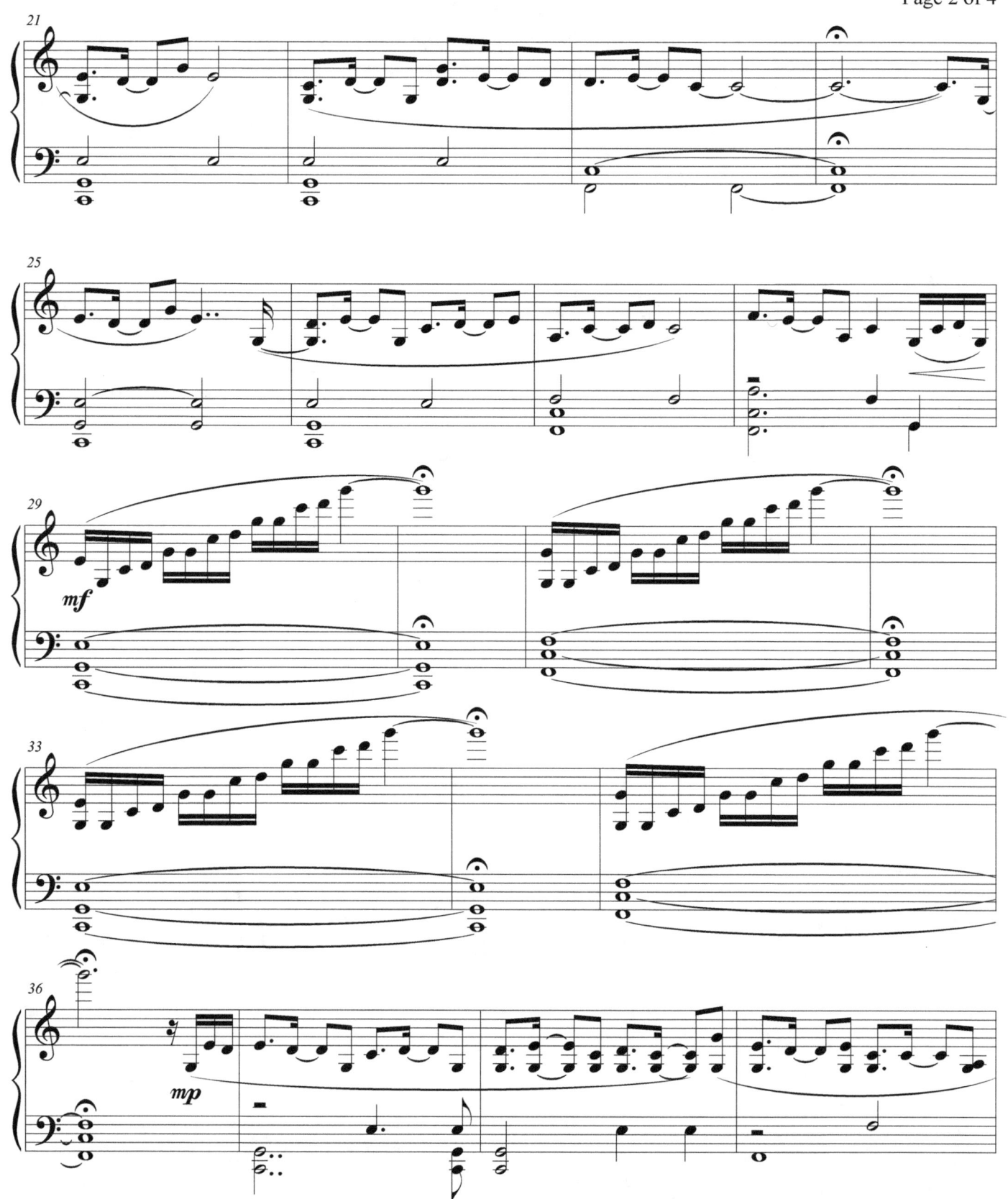

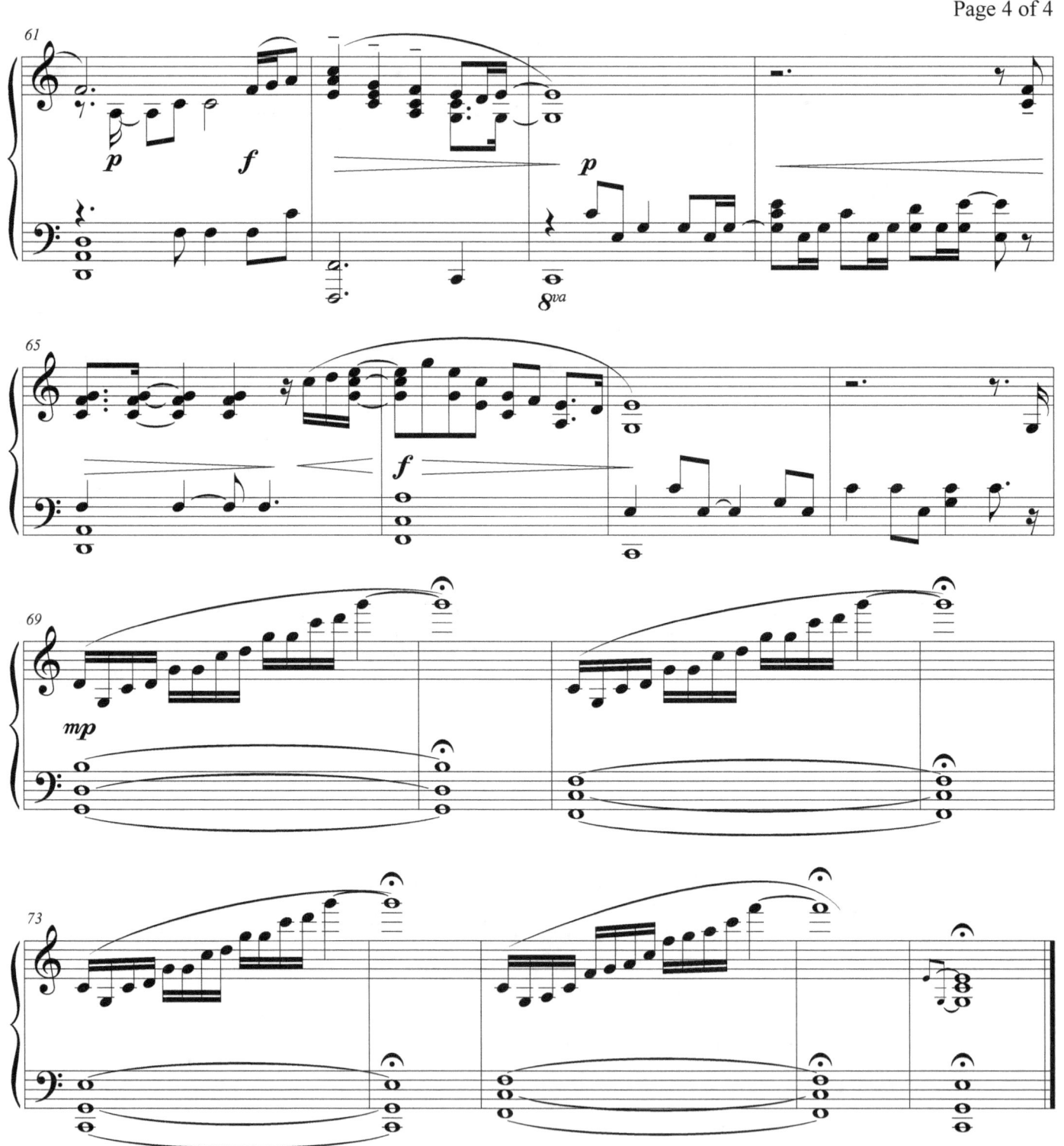

Sands of Time

from the solo piano CD, *Healing Piano of Sedona for massage, yoga and relaxation*
Available from *www.louislandon.com*

LOUIS LANDON

Copyright © 2014 Landon Creative, Inc. (BMI)
International Copyright Secured. All Rights Reserved.

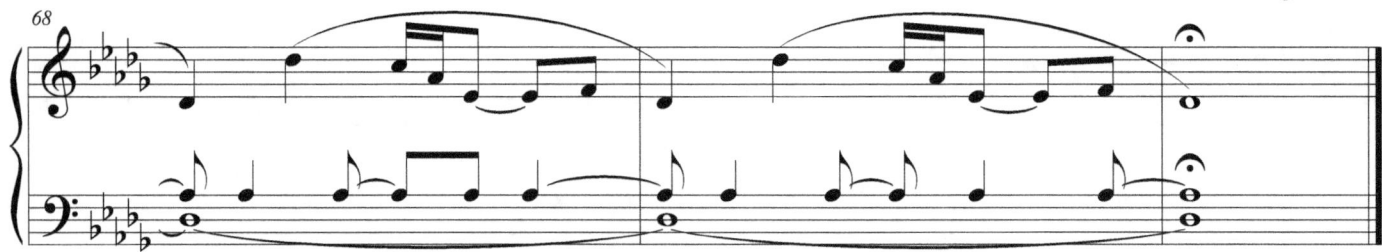

Ascending Souls

from the solo piano CD, *Healing Piano of Sedona for massage, yoga and relaxation*
Available from *www.louislandon.com*

LOUIS LANDON

Child's Pose

from the solo piano CD, *Healing Piano of Sedona for massage, yoga and relaxation*
Available from *www.louislandon.com*

LOUIS LANDON

Copyright © 2014 Landon Creative, Inc. (BMI)
International Copyright Secured. All Rights Reserved.

Harp Goddess

from the solo piano CD, *Healing Piano of Sedona for massage, yoga and relaxation*
Available from *www.louislandon.com*

LOUIS LANDON

Dream Weaver

from the solo piano CD, *Healing Piano of Sedona for massage, yoga and relaxation*
Available from *www.louislandon.com*

LOUIS LANDON

Water Wheel

from the solo piano CD, *Healing Piano of Sedona for massage, yoga and relaxation*
Available from *www.louislandon.com*

LOUIS LANDON

Copyright © 2014 Landon Creative, Inc. (BMI)
International Copyright Secured. All Rights Reserved.

Perseverance

from the solo piano CD, *Healing Piano of Sedona for massage, yoga and relaxation*
Available from *www.louislandon.com*

LOUIS LANDON

Garden of Eden

from the solo piano CD, *Healing Piano of Sedona for massage, yoga and relaxation*
Available from www.louislandon.com

LOUIS LANDON

Into the Depths

from the solo piano CD, *Healing Piano of Sedona for massage, yoga and relaxation*
Available from *www.louislandon.com*

LOUIS LANDON

Soaring

from the solo piano CD, *Healing Piano of Sedona for massage, yoga and relaxation*
Available from www.louislandon.com

LOUIS LANDON

Copyright © 2014 Landon Creative, Inc. (BMI)
International Copyright Secured. All Rights Reserved.

Shangri-La

from the solo piano CD, *Healing Piano of Sedona for massage, yoga and relaxation*
Available from *www.louislandon.com*

LOUIS LANDON

Copyright © 2014 Landon Creative, Inc. (BMI)
International Copyright Secured. All Rights Reserved.

ISBN 978-0-9863062-8-0